THIS NOTEBOOK BELONGS TO :

Made in United States
Troutdale, OR
01/02/2025

27519778R10070